REMOVING
The Veil

CARRADINE FRANKLIN HAWKINS KORNEGAY PINKNEY

Volume 1

REMOVING
The Veil

Harris Publishing Co. ISBN: 0-9760116-9-7

www.harrispubco.com

Printed in the United States of America

www.takingoffthemask.com

Edited by Robert Pinkney

Contents

INTRODUCTION

Six years ago, in the midst of our first worship encounter the Lord spoke and said "TAKE THE MASK OFF." So let me ask, do you have on a mask? And if so, what kind of mask do you have on? What is it that keeps you hiding behind your mask, and why won't you take it off? It is time to be transparent with God, learn how to apply the scriptures to our daily walk and experience emotional healing.

Are you hurting? Are you confused or frustrated? As you begin to read through the pages of this book, don't look to find some "deep" revelation because it's not here. Don't look to find a quick fix to a problem; it's not here. One thing is for certain: as you begin to examine what is written, your issue will find you. Hebrews 4:12 says that the Word of God is sharper than any two-edged sword and that it can discern the very thoughts and intentions of our heart. It's time to take the masks off and get real.

It has been amazing to see and experience the number of things we as Christians try so hard to hide, often not realizing that healing and deliverance for that issue is just around the corner waiting to be revealed. II Corinthians 13:5 (TNIV) says, "**Examine yourselves** to see whether you are in the faith; **test yourselves**..."

Join with us as we remove the veils and build up God's kingdom. He wants to perform surgery and heal us from the inside out. We must not be afraid to confront our issues in order to go where He wants to take us and do what He has called and appointed us to do. We found that as we began to uncover areas that were hidden in the recesses of our lives, one thing led to another. We have masked depression and rejection, and we have hidden behind pasted smiles, jumping, shouting and speaking in tongues. During our studies, we discovered that deception was present in the book of Genesis; it is present today and is being exposed by the Truth. God is showing us where we as Christians have become self-righteous and haughty and He is holding us accountable to the vision to which He has called us.

Hebrews 4:12 finds emphasis more and more as we realize that God's Word is reaching into those deep places of our lives. God wants to teach us what it really means to be in right standing with Him and how to walk in deliverance. We must put on the whole armor of God because if any portion of our armor is missing, the enemy will try to capitalize on those areas in our lives where we are weak. We realize that removing these veils may make us uncomfortable. The enemy wants us to have the same response that Adam and Eve had when deception entered into their lives: they hid themselves. However, God is shining the light on our darkness so that we may be delivered.

REMOVING *The* *Veil*

of Deception

Co-Pastor Brenda Carradine

"So it came about in the morning that, behold, it was Leah! And he said to Laban, "What is this you have done to me? Was it not for Rachel that I served with you? Why then have you deceived me?" Genesis 29:25 (NASB)

Oh my God! How in the world did Laban scam a man like Jacob? Well, incidentally, this is the whole matter concerning deception. Deception is the skill of successfully presenting a falsity as though it were actually real. Webster defines deception as "the act of deceiving another; or a misleading falsehood." In addition to this definition, words such as untruth, false pretense, hocus-pocus, slickness, trickery and fraudulence also encompass it. By and large, deception causes grief, and when it is fully played out, it destroys both the deceived and the deceiver. Of all the schemes of Satan, deception rocks the very core of its victim's spirit. Deception leaves its victims crippled and paralyzed by contempt.

Last year a dear friend of mine (named Trae) decided to buy herself a brand new 2010 Mercedes Benz. She inscribed on her license plate, the slogan "b-traed." I was curious as to why she would select such a painful word for such a beautiful car; so I asked her. Although she did not reveal her reasoning in detail, I knew the slogan suggested she was playing out the revenge of past deceptions. Truly, one of the hallmark signs of the end times is an increase in the operation of the spirit of deception. Deception is the primary tactic of the spirit of the anti-Christ.

Consequently, in order for Satan to deceive you, he has to convince you to believe the lie. Interestingly enough, Satan doesn't remove or displace truth. No, he simply veils the truth by distorting "proper" judgment and discernment. Deception thwarts the perception and spiritual visibility of its victims. Therefore, we must pray for spiritual discernment. I admonish you to covet this gift with all your heart. The Bible says a time will "come when even the elect could be deceived." The elect, my friend, are the chosen people of God! Therefore, every decision and encounter you contemplate must be bathed in prayer and intercession. Jeremiah 17:9 (NASV) states, "The heart is more deceitful than all else; and is desperately sick; who can understand it?" Believers, no one can walk in the spirit and the flesh at the same time. Learn how to unveil and unmask the enemy's deceptive tactics by abiding in the Word of God and walking in the Spirit. Beloved, put on the whole armor of God: in doing so, you will be able to stand against the wiles of the devil!

Dear Lord, keep me far from deception. Show me when men's motives are unjust. Teach me to consistently be alert and watchful. Guard my heart so I do not fall into temptation. Condition my senses so I am aware of demonic intrusion. Bequeath a spirit of discernment upon me. In Jesus' Name. Amen.

REMOVING *The* *Veil* | of Depression

Evangelist Yolonda Y. Franklin

At this moment, you may be discouraged about life, which to you may appear to be an endless, tragic treadmill, not really worth living or having. Perhaps, your view of life is that it holds nothing for you, that it is only a lousy trip. You may even be caught in the throes of self-pity, thinking that nobody loves you or cares whether you live or die. On top of that, you may be doing your best to hide those insecurities from others. If this is your plight, you are struggling with the veil of depression.

Depression is a widespread condition affecting millions of people, Christians and non-Christians alike. Those suffering from depression can experience intense feelings of sadness, anger, hopelessness, fatigue, and a variety of other symptoms. They may feel useless and even suicidal, losing interest in things and people they once enjoyed. Depression is often triggered by life circumstances, such as job loss, death of a loved one or divorce. It can also result from psychological problems, such as abuse or low self-esteem.

However, depression is never the will of God for Christians. In fact, the Bible instructs us to be filled with joy and praise (Philippians 4:4; Romans 15:11), which is the opposite of depression. Therefore, in the midst of your despair, doubt, frustration, or hopelessness, I want you to realize that Jesus Christ offers you another view of life, one that is truly beautiful. Notice His special words to us: "I have come that they may have life, and that they may have *it* more abundantly" (John 10:10 NKJV). With these words, Jesus lifts life above the physical realm, assuring us that our lives have a divine and eternal quality. The Bible further declares that we were created in the very image and likeness of God. You can be certain that since God made us like Himself, our lives have destiny, tremendous meaning, and purpose. It is only after you change your perspective to match Jesus' perspective that you are ready to combat depression. What follows is a discussion of those steps necessary to permanently remove the veil of depression.

1. **Commit yourself to complete repentance, change, and recovery.** Change, especially as it relates to repentance, is necessary to whip depression. David provides a great example of using change in this manner. To conceal his adulterous affair with Bathsheba, and her ensuing pregnancy, David attempted to arrange a sexual encounter between her and husband Uriah. His intent was to frame Uriah for the pregnancy. When his efforts failed, he had Uriah killed. Sin hurts our relationship with our Heavenly Father, which leads to depression. Therefore, David became unhappy,

disheartened and depressed, as a result of his sin. At one point, he lamented: "When I kept silent, my bones grew old through my groaning all the day long. For day and night Your hand was heavy upon me; My vitality was turned into the drought of summer." (Psalm 32:3-4).

However, David did not allow depression to have the final say. After a confrontation with Nathan, David chose repentance and change. In his repentance, he learned, "The righteous cry out, and the LORD hears, and delivers them out of all their troubles. The LORD is near to those who have a broken heart, and saves such as have a contrite spirit" (Psalm 34:17-18 NKJV). David's repentance came with a prayer for change. Psalm 51:10, 12 (ASV) contains that prayer: "Create in me a clean heart, O God; and renew a right spirit within me. Restore to me the joy of your salvation; and uphold me with a willing spirit." The good news of these scriptures is that deliverance awaits every depressed individual who calls on the Lord.

You will do well to follow David's example. Instead of succumbing to the pressure of circumstances, you must be willing to give them to God and move forward! You cannot remain in the same place without risking your life (spiritually but sometimes naturally as well). Certainly, God desires more for you. Deliverance is available to you right now even as you read these words. I speak to your broken spirit and command it to LIVE! Your purpose is also at stake. Your ability to minister to others hinges on your decision regarding depression. So get up and press ahead, remembering that the Lord will turn your mourning into dancing and replace your sackcloth with gladness (see Psalm 30:11 NKJV).

2. **Commit yourself to prayer and fasting.** In times of trouble or despair, we must position ourselves like Hezekiah. II Kings 20 reveals that when Hezekiah received news of his impending death, from the prophet Isaiah, he turned to the Lord. His prayer necessitated Isaiah's abrupt return with the following response from God: "Thus says the Lord, the God of David your father: I have heard your PRAYER, I have seen your tears. Behold I will heal you. On the third day you shall go up to the house of the Lord and I will add fifteen years to your life" (II Kings 20:5-6 emphasis added).

As Hezekiah demonstrated, prayer is our direct line to our Heavenly Father, and it changes things! In prayer, we get to plead our case. For Hezekiah, that meant reminding God of his devotion to righteousness. For us New Testament believers, that means coming in faith through the Blood of Jesus to lay hold of the promises of God's Word. Among those promises is freedom from issues that lead to depression. We must also resolve to stay in the battle to take back everything the enemy has stolen, including the joy that prevails over depression. Hezekiah did not let illness get the best of him. Instead, he petitioned God, and God answered by adding years to his life. Likewise, God wants to extend His grace and mercy to us.

3. **Commit yourself to building a stronger more personal relationship with your Heavenly Father.** This is not easy for someone suffering from depression. At the low point in life, it is hard to build anything, but it is possible. In I Samuel Chapter 2, Hannah gave us an example. She continually trusted and grew closer to God, so much so that she made a vow to give back the very thing she was asking from God. She persisted in prayer despite how she felt. God looked on Hannah and opened her

womb, from which she gave birth to a son. She kept her promise and gave him over to the Lord. God granted Hannah's desire because of her faith, her relationship and her commitment to him. When we, through prayer and faith, continually build our relationship with God, He will also give us the desires of our heart.

4. **Commit your entire body to God**. "They went to a place called Gethsemane, and Jesus said to his disciples, sit here while I pray. He took Peter, James and John along with him, and he began to be deeply distressed and troubled. My soul is overwhelmed with sorrow to the point of death, he said to them. Stay here and keep watch. Going a little farther, he fell to the ground and prayed that if possible the hour might pass from him. Abba, Father, he said, everything is possible for you. Take this cup from me. Yet not what I will, but what you will" (Mark 14:32-42 TNIV emphasis added).

From the preceding passage of scripture, we find that even Jesus met depression head-on, as He considered laying down his life for the world. This is an important point because the way Jesus handled this issue is exactly the way we should handle it. Jesus' answer to depression was simply to succumb to the will of the Father. He prayed, "If it be possible, let this cup pass from me, nevertheless, not as I will but as You will" (Matthew 26:39 NKJV). Put yourself in Jesus' position. What if you, despite your innocence, were condemned to die so that the guilty could live? How would you take it? Would you be able to stand like Jesus, through hurt, pain, and brokenness?

Instead of submitting to depression, Jesus submitted to the will of the Father. We can resist depression as well. However, like Jesus, we must die to our flesh and commit our entire body to God. Jesus gave up the fleshly body to inherit an everlasting seat at the right hand of the Father. We also can succeed and inherit everlasting life when we totally commit ourselves over to the will of God! Think about this: if Jesus had not resisted the sorrow that assaulted Him in the Garden of Gethsemane, He would have been unable to fulfill his destiny of redeeming humanity from the kingdom of darkness. In other words, depression threatens destiny and can therefore never be taken lightly.

5. **Commit to renew your mind to focus on God.** Satan's plan is to conquer our minds. If he can keep us in a depressed state of mind, he wins. Satan knows that if our minds are not focused on God, we are unstable in all our ways and will do anything contrary to the Word of God. We must therefore renew our minds daily, and continue to have our minds focused on God and what He has to say about us. The Bible tells us exactly how to do that: "Finally, brethren, whatsoever things are true, whatsoever things are honest, whatsoever things are just, whatsoever things are pure, whatsoever things are lovely, whatsoever things are of good report; if there be any virtue, and if there be any praise, think on these things" (Philippians 4:8 KJV). Everyday Satan wars against the mind because it is the hub from which everything functions.

The story of Samson and Delilah (see Judges 16:1-21) is a good example. Delilah relentlessly harassed Samson to get him to reveal the secret of his strength. Samson's battle involved his mind, as he had to decide where to direct his focus. Unfortunately, he focused on Delilah rather than on the consequences of disclosing the source of his strength. His mind was definitely not on God, his purpose and his destiny. One thing to always remember is that the duty of Satan is to steal, kill and destroy (see John 10:10). He will stop at NOTHING until he accomplishes his goal.

Nevertheless, continually focusing on the Word of God will strengthen your mind and consequently thwart the enemy's plans. The Word will keep you as it did Jesus when he was led into the wilderness and tempted by Satan (see Matthew 4:1-11). Because Jesus kept his mind focused the Word of God, He was able to resist all the devil's temptations. I can assure you Satan will come against you, but he does not have to win! You can stop him by obeying the mandate of Romans 12:2, "And be not conformed to this world: but be ye transformed by the renewing of your mind, that ye may prove what is that good, and acceptable, and perfect, will of God." The good, acceptable and perfect will of God does not include depression.

6. **Commit to taking care of yourself; stay focused on God and never give up!** I Kings 19:1-4 TNIV "Now Ahab told Jezebel everything Elijah had done and how he had killed all the prophets with the sword. So Jezebel sent a messenger to Elijah to say, May the gods deal with me, be it ever so severely, if by this time tomorrow I do not make your life like that of one of them Elijah was afraid and ran for his life. When he came to Beersheba in Judah, he left his servant there, while he himself went a day's journey into the desert. He came to a broom tree, sat down under it and prayed that he might die. I have had enough, LORD, he said. Take my life; I am no better than my ancestors."

Elijah experienced fatigue and depression right after a great spiritual victory: the defeat of the prophets of Baal and the victory of the God of Israel. Even great victories can lead to depression, if we take our focus off God. Elijah momentarily turned his focus from God to himself. However, self-focus could not sustain him in the face of Jezebel's threats. Consequently, Elijah became so depressed that he wanted to give up and die. His self-pitying rant is recorded in I Kings

19:10 (TNIV), "… I have been very zealous for the LORD God Almighty. The Israelites have rejected your covenant, torn down your altars, and put your prophets to death with the sword. I am the only one left, and now they are trying to kill me too." He walked away from the place of victory into the place of fear because he lost his focus. However, God used a regimen to strengthen Elijah and refocus his attention, thereby leading him out of depression. That regimen included rest, nutrition and encouragement. This is a regimen you can also use to get over the humps of life.

In essence, depression is an attack that expresses itself through mood changes, physical functions, and loss of interest or pleasure, feelings of guilt or low self-esteem. As a veil, it masks or covers the truth about our identity in Christ Jesus, and it keeps us from being real with others. The good news is that in Christ, we have the victory over the veil of depression. This section detailed a number of steps which can be taken to prevent or overcome depression. Each step involves a commitment beyond what many care to make. However, to those who understand the toll of depression, no commitment is too great.

No one likes to admit to having a struggle with depression, nor do they relish asking for help when they need it. However, the devil uses the stigma of depression to keep believers in bondage. Therefore, isolation is not an option for those desiring deliverance. Among other things, fellowshipping with people who are rooted and grounded in the Lord can provide the support to take the necessary steps to freedom.

Above all things, remember that compassion is a great prescription for depression. Consciously renouncing self-absorption is essential, as feelings of depression are often resolved when those suffering with depression move the focus from themselves to *Christ* and others. Though deliberately choosing joy is not always easy, it is possible through prayer, Bible study, and fellowship among believers, confession, forgiveness and counseling. It is time for you to do whatever it takes to defeat depression, once and for all. Are you ready?

Father, in the name of Jesus, I come before your throne boldly today, knowing that I am a child of God and I belong to you. Remove this veil of depression from me. It is my desire to serve you with gladness and to praise you with my whole heart. I completely surrender to you today knowing that you will turn my mourning into joy and nothing can separate me from the love of God, which is in Christ Jesus our Lord. In Jesus' Name, AMEN!

REMOVING *The* *Veil* | of Lack

Elder Karen F. Hawkins

A short time ago, I was driving up the interstate to the airport discussing an upcoming move with the Lord. In discussing the increase in responsibilities as a result of this move, I had concerns about depending on others. After sharing my feelings with the Lord He basically asked me if I was depending on people or Him. He informed me that I couldn't even depend on my paycheck because my employer could declare bankruptcy at any time. It was clear from my conversation with God that He was the only One on whom I could depend. So, it stands to reason, that if my dependence is on God, I lack nothing.

I have a testimony that will drive home my point. I am basically an introverted person. People don't normally discern that about me because God places me in situations and around people that pull on my gifts to such a degree that I am forced from my shell. However, if I had my way, I would fade into the background. One reason for my shyness is that for a good part of my life, I didn't like myself. I felt I was ugly and undesirable compared to my friends and others around me. From my vantage point, I simply did not measure up. My relationships only served to reinforce those thoughts of what I felt I "lacked".

When I was 37 years old, God began rummaging through my garbage can of issues I carried around. It was a major clean up in every area of my life, and it resulted in a brand new perspective. I began to see myself as He saw me. I discovered that, despite what I thought I did not have, I am all right and in God, I lack nothing. At that point, I began surveying my life and realized that whenever I faced so-called lack, God was always there to satisfy my needs. For example, when I felt I lacked friendship, God put people in my life. When I felt I lacked love, my daughter would come home and hug my neck. Moreover, at work, God opened doors of opportunity that others could not get. He gave me favor in unlikely places and with people not known for showing favor. And when I lacked enough money to pay my bills, He gave me a strategy to which my creditors agreed and which brought me out of debt. God put people, places and things in place to fulfill what I "thought" I was missing.

The whole idea behind the veil of lack is to counterfeit the place of prosperity and sufficiency in the life of the believer. The plan of the enemy is to get us to accept the idea that God will not always provide for our needs. If we buy into that lie, we negate the power and provisions that God has made for us. I initially had a hard time with this lesson because it brought me face to face with my own thoughts about lack, especially given my current state of transition at that time. However, I learned to see things in a different light. I learned to look beyond myself (my thoughts and ways) to become totally dependent on Him. That's what we all must do. Even when we do not have what we need, we must maintain our dependency on and our faith in God regardless of how things appear.

God's will is that we prosper—not lack—in every area of our lives. III John 2 makes this abundantly clear: "Beloved, I wish above all things that you may *prosper* and be in health, even as your soul prospers" (Emphasis added). In this verse, prosperity encompasses a course of conduct or a way or manner of thinking, feeling, or deciding that brings success. In other words, prosperity begins in the soul (our mind, will and emotions) and affects every area of life. Therefore, the counterfeit or opposite of prosperity involves a course of conduct or a way or manner of thinking, feeling or deciding that opens the door to lack or a poverty mentality. Lack also begins in the soul. Incidentally, it involves more than financial poverty. Poverty of spirit, knowledge, understanding, wisdom, relationship and health are all examples of lack. People can also experience a lack of opportunities, a lack of courage, and a lack of faith; the list is potentially endless.

Removing the veil of lack requires a complete change of perspective or mindset (attitude and disposition). In other words, we must change the way we think, believe and the things we do in order to remove this veil. Essentially, we must renew our minds to agree with the Word of God. In that way, we would be able to prove prosperity—i.e., the absence of lack—as part of the good, acceptable and perfect will of God (see Romans 12:2). Simply put, there is no unveiling of any falsity, lack or otherwise, without a consistent application of the Word of God. Knowing the will of God is the first step towards deliverance from lack. Therefore, let's review a few more scriptures that clearly show that lack is "not" the will of God.

Psalm 84:11 states, "For the LORD God is a sun and shield: the LORD will give grace and glory: no good thing will He withhold from them that walk uprightly." According to this scripture, God keeps the upright well supplied. So what "good thing" is God withholding from us? We know also from Philippians 4:19 that "God supplies all of our needs according to His riches in glory by Christ Jesus." Therefore, what "NEED" has He not supplied? Not only does He supply every need, but He also supplies every need in its entirety. A full supply is a far cry from lack. Furthermore, according to Matthew 7:7-8, the will of God for prosperity is far-reaching. It is for all those who persistently ask, seek or knock. Any limitation, where prosperity is concerned, is self-imposed.

Perhaps the greatest testimony against lack is contained in Psalm 23. This psalm is direct in its claim that because the Lord is our Shepherd, we have no lack. Every successive verse affirms the Lord's provision and deliverance from lack. The Good Shepherd leads us into life-giving pastures, causes us to rest besides peaceful waters and restores our souls. Remember that the soul is where prosperity begins; so a restored soul is definitely a prosperous soul. Even in difficult times, the presence of the Shepherd is so reassuring that there is no fear of evil. Moreover, the Shepherd comforts, vindicates and anoints to overflowing. According to verse 6, "surely goodness and mercy shall follow [us] all the days of [our] lives." When we follow the Word of God, nothing is missing.

Our concentrated effort should be to do whatever is necessary to remove lack from our lives. If we were to examine ourselves, we are sure to find lack in some area, likely in more than one. Lack hinders us from fulfilling God's plan for our lives. So it is time for us to remove the veil of lack once and for all!

Therefore, I want to give a scriptural foundation on how to remove the veil of lack. James 1:5-8 provides an important key to removing lack. Though it focuses on wisdom, it is applicable to every area of our lives where lack is a concern. It reads as follows: "If any of you lack wisdom, let him ask of God, that giveth to all men liberally, and upbraids not; and it shall be given him. But let him ask in faith, nothing wavering. For he that wavers is like a wave of the sea driven with the wind and tossed. For let not that man think that he shall receive any thing of the Lord. A double minded man is unstable in all his ways."

This scripture makes two important points that are necessary for removing lack. First, the person suffering from lack must ask God for the thing he lacks. To Christians, that should be a no-brainer. However, we often take matters into our own hands, involving God only as a last resort. When we ask upfront, God immediately becomes involved in our situation, and the journey out of lack is shorter and less exasperating. God will always give us a strategy when we ask. This is exactly what I experienced when I sought God from the onset for a plan to pay off my creditors. Second, we must ask in faith, without wavering. I John 5:14-15 guarantees answered prayer when we pray according to the will of God. The scripture states that "this is the confidence we have in approaching God: that if we ask "anything" according to His will He hears us. And if we know that He hears us – whatever we ask – we know that we have what we asked of Him."

21

This is exactly why I spent time establishing from scripture that lack is not the will of God and we can pray about removing lack without double-mindedness.

No discourse on lack would be complete without a discussion on words. Mark 11:22-24 is a case in point. Some time after Jesus cursed the fig tree, Peter noticed that the tree had withered and called it to Jesus' attention. Jesus' response to Peter's observation is recorded in Mark 11:22 "Have faith in God." Jesus goes on in verses 23 and 24 to say "For assuredly, I say to you, whoever says to this mountain, Be removed and be cast into the sea, and does not doubt in his heart, but believes that those things he says will be done, he will have whatever he says. Therefore I say to you, whatever things you ask when you pray, believe that you receive *them,* and you will have *them...*" (NKJV) Jesus revealed an important principle concerning our words and answered prayer. Though it is important to pray in faith, it is equally important to watch the words we say after we pray. This is especially important during times of waiting when we are tempted to complain about the lack we see. However, when we speak words that agree with God's perspective of lack, we reinforce our faith in God, which puts us in a position to receive.

The bottom line is that we can have exactly what we say, mainly because what we consistently say is what we believe. The Bible states that whatever is in your heart determines what you say (see Matthew 12:34). Likewise Proverbs 27:19 (NKJV) states "As in water face *reflects* face, so a man's heart *reveals* the man." That is to say, our words reflect what we believe in our heart. So if we want to come out of lack into provision, we must put the right words in our mouth. For instance, instead of speaking of our lack, we speak of our Shepherd in whom we have no lack. Instead of worrying over our needs, we speak that our needs are met according to Philippians 4:19. Proverbs 18:21 states "death and life are in the power of the tongue." So your power to come out of lack is in your mouth. You must deliberately and consistently use it to forge your way out. I am not suggesting that making confessions of faith is the sole key to removing the veil of lack. However, I am saying that it is a very important key that cannot be overlooked—not if you are serious about removing the veil.

Another way to combat lack is to rightly discern the Body of Christ. I Corinthians 12 includes a discussion of spiritual gifts as well as how the members of the Body of Christ are supposed to relate to each other. God has set us in different places in the Body and has given us different gifts. Often, what one believer lacks, another believer has. Therefore, we should be able to come together as a body where each joint supplies the need of another. In essence, we must learn to support and depend on each other. I opened this chapter by emphasizing the importance of relying on God. However, that does not mean that we do not depend on each other; it only means that we do not place people in the position of God.

Matthew 6:33 offers additional insight into abolishing lack. It instructs us to "seek first the kingdom of God, and His righteousness; and all these things (what we need as well as what we want) shall be added unto [us]." In one translation, the kingdom of God is referred to as God's way of doing, and righteousness is referred as God's way of being right. This involves perspective and action. We adopt God's perspective of right and wrong as our own, and we take action based on that perspective. For example, we agree with God's perspective that tithing is right, and based on that perspective, we take action to tithe. In this way, we give first place to the kingdom of God and His righteousness. When we do that, lack is no longer a problem.

In conclusion, the Bible is clear that lack is not the will of God. Yet, many of us struggle with lack in some area of life. The problem with lack is that it can interfere with our destiny. God has, however, made a way of escape through His Word. It is time that we take that way of escape and remove the veil of lack from our lives. When we do so, we prove the good, perfect and acceptable will of God. We become visible examples of the goodness of God and ultimately become drawing cards for those outside the Kingdom of God. The bottom line is lack must go. Join me in the following prayer of praise, petition and commitment to follow the Word of God so that our lives may once and for all be lack free.

Heavenly Father, we thank You for Your love, grace and mercy towards us. Help us Lord to remove the scales from our eyes so that we are able to see clearly. Lord, we do ask for Your wisdom and guidance so that we can walk uprightly before You. Forgive us for not fully trusting in You and believing in Your Word and the provisions that You have made for us. Lord, You have instructed us to capture every thought that opposes Your Word and to make our thoughts obedient to Christ. Father we thank You for giving us the courage and strength to stand against every thought that does not line up with Your Word. Help us to recognize Your hand in our lives so that we can see clearly that in YOU, we lack no good thing because You said You would provide for all of our needs according to Your riches in glory through Christ Jesus. And now Father, we have understood what You are saying to us. We purpose in our hearts to walk therein so that our lives will bear fruit that will glorify You and defeat every attack of the devil. We come against every stronghold of the mind and will renew our minds through Your Word. Father, we love You and give You thanks. In Jesus' name, we pray. AMEN!

REMOVING *The* *Veil* | of Rejection

Elder Sharon R. Kornegay

Psalm 118: 22 – *"The stone that the builders rejected has now become the chief cornerstone."*

Reject: To refuse to accept, consider, submit to, or take for some purpose of use; to refuse to hear, receive or admit.

Imagine what Jesus and others throughout the Bible must have felt when they experienced the spirit of rejection. Rejection results in disallowance, attack, contradiction and feeling unwanted, inadequate or like the proverbial black sheep. Yet, Jesus and other Biblical characters defied the spirit of rejection to accomplish the will of God for their lives. Therefore, Jesus became our example. He does not want us to give credence to the voice of rejection. As everybody experiences rejection, it is vitally important to recognize the traits of rejection so that we are able to realize when the enemy has established a demonic stronghold. Otherwise, we will never be able to be all that God created us to be because of an inability to accept and fully comprehend how much God loves and cares for us.

So much can be said about the veil of rejection that I am not able to cover in this chapter, because rejection has limitless causes and consequences. Most of the time, the spirit of rejection enters during childhood and sometimes lies dormant and is not acknowledged until later. It is also possible for rejection to enter prior to childhood if a pregnant woman, bound by the spirit of rejection, voices negative comments that provide an invitation for demonic entry. Life and death is in the power of the tongue. He that loves them will eat the fruit thereof (see Proverbs 18:21).

Until recently, I did not recognize the firm grip of rejection in my life. The spirit of rejection entered my life during childhood. I was constantly teased and sometimes excluded from the "in-crowd". I also witnessed turmoil at home, sometimes hearing distressful words that wreaked havoc in my life. I even recall wearing a turquoise t-shirt with a picture of a black sheep. When I think about it, I had become a walking advertisement for the devil. Without speaking it out of my mouth, I had actually embraced the spirit of rejection. Because rejection was never dealt with, I brought that same spirit to adulthood and into my relationships with others. I became bitter and resentful until I committed my life to pleasing God rather than men.

Rejection causes hurt, and hurt people hurt others. An unending cycle results unless deliverance takes place in the life of the person demonically oppressed by the spirit of rejection. Because rejection causes deep emotional wounds, those dealing with rejection often wear masks, not wanting others to know about their insecurities. A common mask is overachievement, because those dealing with rejection oftentimes use success as a way to become accepted. Although success sometimes brings acceptance, it does nothing for the root of rejection established during childhood. Others accept less than God's best for them in a marriage, friendship or other relationship. Because they are accustomed to rejection, they become consumed with performance-based servitude.

The spirit of rejection attaches itself to the part of our nature that wants to be received and accepted. People dealing with rejection find it hard to fit in with others, likely because they have experienced abuse in some form or another. Rejection has various sources: divorce issues, infidelity of a spouse, rebellion, sexual abuse and even parent or sibling rivalries—just to name a few. If not delivered from the effects and pain resulting from the spirit of rejection, people will always face issues of distrust, fear, paranoia, self-pity and, in some instances, promiscuity. Other fruits of rejection include envy, jealousy, pride, resentment, schizophrenia, self-identification issues, self-hatred and self-unforgiveness, and feelings of unworthiness. Oftentimes, people dealing with rejection find fault and point fingers at others. Quite honestly, rejection is really just another form of emotional abuse.

Rejection gives entrance to all kinds of demonic strongholds. The enemy always distorts truth in order to strengthen his influence in our lives. He uses rejection as a form of bondage to keep people on lock-down. Deliverance requires forgiveness, prayer, renewal of the mind through the application, study of God's Word and much fasting. People can never be delivered from the veil of rejection unless they fully understand who they are in Christ Jesus. The Bible implies in John 17:23 that we are loved with the same love that the Father has for Jesus Himself. We have to know "WHOSE" we are in order to know "WHO" we are. We will never know whose we are if we do not take the time to read the Word and apply it to our daily lives. We have to receive God's love; otherwise, the rejection cycle will be unending.

Satan works through rejection because it is rooted in deception and lies. He himself cannot receive truth because truth is not in him. He uses the spirit of rejection to keep people isolated and bound to the belief that they are unloved and unwanted. Satan uses rejection everywhere: on the job, in the home, in political and social settings and even in the church. There are no geographical or human barriers as far as the spirit of rejection is concerned. As a result, people often find themselves tormented by thoughts of abandonment and defeat. The spirit of rejection can also lead to suicide.

There is an old saying, "Sticks and stones may break my bones, but words will never hurt me." There is nothing farther from the truth. Words do hurt. Words are very powerful and meaningful. Nothing bothers me more than to have people say something hurtful to me. However, in all honesty, we all have been both initiators and partakers of rejection. Rejection, through words, is an everyday occurrence. It is present in relationships, marriages, and the list goes on and on. Think about it. Have you ever wanted to be chosen to be a member of a team and were not selected? How did you feel? I remember playing games like red-light, hopscotch, and softball during childhood. I would sometimes be the last person chosen to be on the team, if chosen at all. I used to walk away, feeling broken, crushed and less adequate than others.

I have also experienced rejection as a seasoned and mature Christian. For example, it took me a long time to let others in the Church know that God had blessed me with gifts, talents and abilities that could be used to enhance the worship service because of the fear of rejection. I would sit down and try to hide out without being noticed. Yet from the pew, I would feel empty and unfulfilled because I knew what God had anointed and called me to contribute to His kingdom. Over the years, I learned that rejection is very common in the church, especially in choir settings. We have to realize that the enemy used to be the worship leader, and he operates through jealousy and manipulation because we are now doing what he used to do. Regardless of what others say or think about you and the gifts that God has deposited in your life, push forward and work the works of Him that sent you while it is day, for the night is coming and then no man will be able to work (see John 9:4). It is time to be about the Father's business.

Rejection in any form can hurt. Let me ask you a question. What is your issue of rejection? Have you ever even thought about it? Perhaps rejection came into your life through the lack of love from a parent or spouse. Perhaps you have been adopted and cannot understand why your parents gave you away. Maybe rejection entered through a bad marriage, relationship, or racism. It does not matter your age or where you were born, the color of your skin or how tall or skinny you are, rejection can occur in your life. Whatever the source, the blood of Jesus is sufficient to deliver all from the strongholds of rejection. There is nothing too hard for God, and we can be made whole.

Jesus witnessed the spirit of rejection in His own life. He stood when He could have very easily sat down and quit. The Bible says that "He was despised and rejected by mankind, a man of suffering, and familiar with pain. Like one from whom people hide their faces he was despised, and we held him in low esteem" (Isaiah 53:3 NKJV). Not only was Jesus rejected from those who did not believe that He was the Son of God, but those who walked alongside Him in ministry also rejected him. God's love was affirmed in His life, and He would not let anything separate Him from the will of the Father.

The Biblical character Joseph experienced rejection as well. He did not ask for it, nor did he do anything to deserve it. Joseph's brothers beat, mocked and scorned him. They were always plotting and trying to figure out a way to attack and hurt him. His brothers stripped him of his most prized possession, his coat of many colors. Joseph was sold into slavery for little or nothing. Nevertheless, Joseph responded to rejection the God kind of way. He did not allow the spirit of rejection to change who God created Him to be.

Moses, Paul and many others in the Bible also experienced the spirit of rejection. Imagine what the woman who was caught in adultery felt like (see John 8:1-11). She was made a public spectacle by religious folk. It is not too often that we take the time to think about all that she must have endured. Have you ever wondered why the man who committed the act of adultery with her did not receive the same treatment? Nobody dragged him out in front of others to be shamed and stoned. Nothing hurts more than to be the talk of the town in a negative way. Think about the opposition she must have experienced when she went into a public place and saw others gathered around looking at her. I am certain it was not pretty.

How do we combat and remove the veil of rejection? We must renounce the spirit of rejection in the name of Jesus Christ. As we cry out to God and trust Him to walk us through, we will be victorious (see Matthew 21:42). The Bible declares in Psalm 34:17-20: "The righteous cry out, and the LORD hears them; He delivers them from all their troubles. The LORD is close to the brokenhearted and saves those who are crushed in spirit. The righteous may have many troubles, but the LORD delivers them from them all; He protects all their bones, not one of them will be broken." We have to understand that in His sight, we are chosen and precious according to 1 Peter 2:4.

In order to move forward beyond the spirit of rejection, we have to come to grips with the issues in our lives that have hurt and caused us disappointment and pain. We must refuse to isolate ourselves from others. Instead, we must surround our lives with people who are mature and sound in the Word of God. It is important that we not get what I call the "shutdown" syndrome. It is the trick of the enemy to defeat and deter us from accomplishing the will of God for our lives. We must determine to be governed by truth, not by our feelings of abandonment, loneliness or unworthiness. The truth is that we are very valuable to God. We do not have to fear being rejected by God because He loves us. He created us and has said that we are fearfully and wonderfully made.

We must remove the veil of rejection so that we are no longer slaves to it. We must not continue to dwell on past issues that magnify and exalt the victim mentality. Instead, we must realize that Christ wants us to be free. He wants us to be whole. It will also do you good to remember that you are not alone in your rejection. In fact, you are in great company. Jesus tells us in John 15:18 (TNIV), "If the world hates you, keep in mind that it hated me first."

Consider Ephesians 6:10-18, (NIV) "Finally, be strong in the Lord and in His mighty power. Put on the full armor of God, so that you can

31

take your stand against the devil's schemes. For our struggle is not against flesh and blood, but against the rulers, against the authorities, against the powers of this dark world and against the spiritual forces of evil in the heavenly realms. Therefore put on the full armor of God, so that when the day of evil comes, you may be able to stand your ground, and after you have done everything, to stand. Stand firm then, with the belt of truth buckled around your waist, with the breastplate of righteousness in place, and with your feet fitted with the readiness that comes from the gospel of peace. In addition to all this, take up the shield of faith, with which you can extinguish all the flaming arrows of the evil one. Take the helmet of salvation and the sword of the Spirit, which is the word of God. And pray in the Spirit on all occasions with all kinds of prayers and requests. With this in mind, be alert and always keep on praying for all of the Lord's people."

Let me ask you a question. Which piece of this shield do you need in order to stand against the spirit of rejection? I am here to tell you that we need all of it. One of my good friends taught me something about the whole armor of God. She said, "We must put all of it on. Otherwise, the enemy will find our area of vulnerability and attack ferociously." The spirit of rejection wants us to feel sorry for ourselves. It wants us to feel worthless, but Jesus makes us worthy. Through His blood, we have been redeemed from the wounds that rejection brings. We must receive His love for us. Until we receive His love, the enemy will continue to gain access through demonic strongholds of loneliness, lack of self-worth and lack of confidence.

Under the control of the spirit of rejection, you will always find yourself trying to perform better or even to become a perfectionist because your peers or those you deemed important never considered you good enough. However, it's time to close the door to the spirit of rejection. I am learning to receive healing in the areas of my life that were painful. In order to be healed, we must first do a spiritual inventory and put our emotions in check. We must assess where we are in life and why we respond the way we do. Finally, we must allow the Holy Spirit to minister to the areas of our lives where we feel despondent and weak. Do not spend the rest of your life donning the mask of rejection. Take it off and be healed in the name of Jesus Christ.

The Word of God is replete with scriptures that guarantee our deliverance from rejection. In Luke 4:18-19 (TNIV), Jesus proclaimed, "The Spirit of the Lord is on me, because He has anointed me to proclaim good news to the poor. He has sent me to proclaim freedom for the prisoners and recovery of sight for the blind, to set the oppressed free, to proclaim the year of the Lord's favor."

Isaiah prophesied concerning Jesus, "The Spirit of the Lord God is upon me; because the Lord hath anointed me to preach good tidings unto the meek; He hath sent me to bind up the brokenhearted, to proclaim liberty to the captives, and the opening of the prison to them that are bound; to proclaim the acceptable year of the Lord, and the day of vengeance of our God; to comfort all that mourn; to appoint unto them that mourn in Zion, to give unto them beauty for ashes, the oil of joy for mourning, the garment of praise for the spirit of heaviness; that they might be called trees of righteousness, the planting of the Lord, that He might be glorified" (Isaiah 61:1-3 KJV).

Psalm 147:3 (NIV) states, "He heals the brokenhearted and binds up their wounds."

These are promises to us from the Word of God, and God cannot lie. He wants us to live free from the spirit of rejection. It is my prayer that you will renounce the spirit of rejection head on. You can overcome it. God has made us more than conquerors through Christ Jesus. Sin has gripped our hearts far too long. We must go to God in prayer trusting that He is a rewarder of those who diligently seek Him. Jesus said in John 6:37 (NKJV), "All that the Father gives Me will come to Me, and the one who comes to Me I will by no means cast out." Isaiah 49:15-16 (NKJV) also states, "Can a woman forget her nursing child, and not have compassion on the son of her womb? Surely they may forget, yet I will not forget you. See, I have inscribed you on the palms of my hands: Your walls are continually before Me." Romans 8:38-39 (NKJV) further states, "For I am persuaded that neither death nor life, nor angels nor principalities nor powers, nor things present nor things to come, nor height nor depth, nor any other created thing, shall be able to separate us from the love of God which is in Christ Jesus our Lord."

I want to invite you to join with me in prayer against the spirit of rejection.

Heavenly Father, I thank You for removing the veil of deception out of my life. I am more than a conqueror through Christ Jesus. Lord, I thank You for being near to the brokenhearted and saving those who are crushed in spirit. Even when my mother and father or others forsake me, Lord, You will raise me up. Your Son has gone before me and is now with me, never leaving nor forsaking me. Therefore, I will not fear or be dismayed. I choose to forgive those who have rejected and offended me. I receive Your love and thank You for the healing power of the stripes of Jesus. By faith, I am delivered from the veil of rejection and thank You for setting me free. I renounce rejection and uproot it out of my life. I declare that I am being made whole through Christ Jesus' blood that was shed for me. In the name of Jesus Christ I pray, Amen.

REMOVING *The* Veil

of Sickness

Co-Pastor Kimberly Pinkney

Webster defines sickness as a *disorder, weakened or unsound condition.* Webster defines disease as *trouble or a harmful development.* While most people would not normally consider disorders, weaknesses or harmful developments conditions to be desired, there still remains a perspective regarding sickness that keeps many Christians in bondage to sickness and disease. In other words, there is a veil that keeps people blinded to the truth regarding this subject. This perspective does not make sense naturally, let alone spiritually. For example, good parents do not stand idly by while sickness or disease ravages the bodies of their children. Instead, they take whatever measures necessary, including great financial sacrifices, to secure the health of their children.

One would think that a logically sound individual would at least assign to God the attributes of a good parent. In other words, it stands to reason that if parents do not relish in their children's sicknesses, then certainly God takes no delight in the sicknesses of his children. That's just it: the perspective most Christians hold regarding sickness lacks logic—Biblical or otherwise. The bottom line is that there is a veil of sickness that blinds Christians to the will of God concerning sickness. Yet, the Bible is clear, from cover to cover, that sickness is never the will of God for his children. Therefore, the only way to remove this veil is through a careful study of the truth from God's Word. Along those lines, let us examining four questions through the Word of God that reveal God's perspective on this topic, thus removing the veil of sickness and bringing the consistent experience of healing to all who will govern themselves accordingly.

The first question is two-fold: a.) Is it the will of God to heal all sickness and disease; and b.) Is it God's will to heal me? We will examine scriptures to answer this question in the affirmative. In Exodus 15:26, the Lord says about Himself: "I am the Lord who heals you", not the Lord who makes you sick or uses your sickness to teach you or glorify myself. In Exodus 23:25, God again says, "I will take sickness away from the midst of thee". Most people would agree that God does not lie. We should therefore be able to believe that sickness is not His will, for we have His word on it. David testifies concerning God: "He (God) sent His word and healed them, and delivered them from their destructions" (Psalm 107:20). David makes this statement about transgressing fools who cry to God in their trouble. If God would heal and deliver a fool, then certainly He would do as much for his children. Isaiah prophesies concerning Jesus that He has borne our griefs and carried our sorrows and that He was wounded for our transgression, bruised for our iniquities; the chastisement for our peace was upon Him, and by His stripes we are healed (see Isaiah 53:4-5).

Now let's examine the New Testament—a better covenant built on better promises—to see what it says about the will of God regarding healing. Matthew 8:17 is a great place to start. It states, He (Jesus) Himself took our infirmities and bore our sicknesses. This is a fulfillment of Isaiah's prophecy. Isaiah prophesied healing; Jesus fulfilled healing! Galatians 3:13 further states, "Christ has redeemed us from the curse of the law being made a curse for us". Everyone Christian and non-Christians know that sickness is not a good thing. Just think about it, this is the reason we deal with doctors—because we know that sickness is not good, that it is a curse!

Let's examine further. Acts 10:38 states, "How God anointed Jesus of Nazareth with the Holy Spirit and with power who went about doing good and healing all who were oppressed of the devil, for God was with Him". This scripture reveals two things at once: that Jesus is the healer and that Satan is the oppressor, who afflicts people with sickness. In Matthew 8:2-3 (TNIV), the question regarding the will of God concerning healing is answered directly: "And behold, a leper came and worshipped Him, saying, Lord if You are willing, you can make me clean". Another translation reads, Lord if it is your will You can make me clean. Like many Christians today, the leper did not question Jesus' ability to heal; he questioned his will to heal. And what was Jesus' response: "I am willing; be cleansed. Immediately his leprosy was cleansed" (verse 3). Jesus' response to leper should settle this issue for us once and for all. Hebrews 13:8 states, Jesus Christ is the same yesterday, today, and forever. In other words, Jesus' response to the leper is the same to you if you question his will.

These scriptures from both the Old and New Testament clearly show that God wants us healed. Healing has always been the will of God, and that will never change. He is more than willing to heal any person from any sickness or disease regardless of its intensity or longevity. Allow these scriptures to remove the veil of deception and accept once and for all that God's will for you is, and will always be—healing.

The second question involves the origin of sickness. Simply put, does sickness come from God? To answer that question, let's return for a moment to the Garden of Eden. The Garden of Eden is the foundation of human origin. Other than heaven, it is the only place where the perfect will of God is shown—that is, before the fall of mankind. The Garden of Eden is our picture of how God lives and how He wants us to live. That being said, there was no sickness in the Garden of Eden. A careful reading of Genesis 1 and 2 confirms this fact. Sickness does not show up in the experience of humanity until Adam and Eve are expelled from the Garden of Eden.

According to James 1:17, "Every good gift and every perfect gift is from above, and comes down from the Father of lights, with whom there is no variation or shadow of turning". Please resist the temptation to be deep as you ponder the following question: is sickness and disease a good and perfect gift? I don't think so. If we thought it was, we would not consult with a doctor to get rid of it. Otherwise, we would do our best to keep it and do everything in our power to share it with others? When you really think about it, this perspective is absolutely absurd. If you want to know if God has ordained something, look at the Garden of Eden. Better yet, see if you can imagine such a condition in heaven. The bottom line: sickness and disease is not good, not perfect, and therefore not of God.

The third question useful in removing the veil of sickness also concerns the origin of sickness and disease. That question is as follows: Is sickness and disease demonically caused? Although all sicknesses and diseases originate with Satan, they are not all demonically caused. One case where demons were directly involved is the epileptic in Mark 9 (see verses 14-27). We know this to be the case because the child was healed after Jesus cast out a demon. Sometimes, there can be many demons involved. In Mark 5, a legion of demons afflicted a man with multiple personalities. Mental diseases are often demonic in nature. After Jesus cast out the legion of demons, the man was completed restored to his right mind; so much so that the townspeople were astonished.

However, not all sicknesses and diseases are directly caused by demons. The Bible provides several examples where our actions put us in a position where we become vulnerable to sickness and disease. In John 5, Jesus healed a man who had an infirmity for thirty-eight years. Jesus' encounter with the man after his healing is rather telling. He instructed the man: "See, you have been made well. Sin no more, lest a worse thing come upon you". Jesus' words reveal that this man's sickness resulted from his sin. What is important about this principle is that if you can sin and become sick, you can repent and become whole again. This gives you authority over sin. Even when sin is demonically inspired, you still have control because, just as Jesus did with the epileptic, you can take authority over the demon causing sickness in your body.

Disobedience is another causal factor of sickness and disease. In II Kings 5:27 (NKJV), Naaman's leprosy transferred to Gehazi when he, in direct violation of God's will, solicited payment from Naaman in return for his healing. The pronouncement of this curse came from

Elisha himself: "Therefore the leprosy of Naaman shall cling to you and your descendants forever. And he went out from his presence leprous as *white* as snow". This leads me to another causal factor. Sickness and disease can sometimes be curses passed down from generation to generation. However, you must remember that according Galatians 3:13, Christ has redeemed Christians from the curse. Therefore, you don't have to accept generational curses.

Christians also open themselves up to sickness and disease through their words. Proverbs 18:21 (NKJV) states, "Death and life are in the power of the tongue, and those who love it will eat its fruit". When it comes to sickness and disease, we must be careful of what we say because we are judged by our words, and sometimes that judgment affects our bodies. In Miriam's case, her words were stout against Moses, God's chosen leader. As a result, she was stricken with leprosy. Even though God eventually restored Miriam through Moses' prayer, her healing was delayed seven days because she dared to defy Moses' leadership.

The Bible discusses many other causes of sickness and disease. When dealing with your particular situation, it is important to seek God concerning the reason for your condition. Otherwise, you might only experience temporary relief or perhaps no release at all. An evangelist once stated that a doctor would not treat a headache with aspirin if that headache were caused by a brain tumor. In making this statement, she was emphasizing the cause, or root, of a problem must be addressed before the problem can be resolved. Sometimes, you might need to repent in order to receive healing. Other times, you might just need to make a change in your speech, your behavior or your habits. The bottom line is that you have more say-so in your healing than you realize. Know this: when it comes to healing, you are not waiting on God because he has already established His will concerning healing. He is waiting on you to do what it takes to remove the veil of sickness so that you can walk in divine health. After all, it is the God of peace who sanctifies you wholly [preserving] your whole spirit, soul, and body (see I Thessalonians 5:23).

The final question: is sickness and disease caused by nutritional habits? I Timothy 4:4 states, "For every creature of God is good and nothing is to be refused if it is received with thanksgiving". The deception here is that we think that because God said every creature is good, we can eat all things without limit and without moderation. We ignore medical research that consistently connects conditions, such as diabetes, high blood pressure, high cholesterol, and heart disease to improper food consumption. We pray over our food, thinking that the prayer will keep the food from harming us. However, just as you cannot put junk in your gas tank and expect your car to run effectively, you cannot continue to put junk in your body and expect it to run effectively.

By the way, junk means anything that your body is not meant to process. Nutritionists advise us to put organic or living foods in our body. They advise against processed foods, which can build up chemicals that can cause cancer and other serious conditions. As our bodies are temples of the Holy Spirit, we need to do everything we can to take care of them. I am not a nutritionist, so I cannot tell you everything you need to do to take care of your body. However, there is a wealth of knowledge from Christian authors on this subject; you should have no problem discovering how to care for your body, if you are serious. We like to keep it spiritual when it comes to healing, but the truth is that you cannot ignore the natural and expect to be whole physically. To do so would simply keep the veil of sickness in place.

Heavenly Father, we thank You Lord for Your Word that says we have benefits that are fresh and new each morning. We thank You that part of those benefits says that we can have divine health and healing. So we command our bodies to line up with Your Word. We declare sickness and disease have no right or authority to operate in our bodies. You took all of our sickness, disease, grief and sorrows and by Your stripes we are healed. You say that you came that we might have life and life more abundantly. We thank you for an abundant life, In Jesus' Name. Amen!

REMOVING The *Veil* | of the Victim

Elder Karen F. Hawkins

Removing the Victim's Veil is centered on the story of Hannah found in I Samuel 1:1-17. Let's look at it:

> ¹ *Now there was a certain man of Ramathaim Zophim, of the mountains of Ephraim, and his name was Elkanah the son of Jeroham, the son of Elihu, the son of Tohu, the son of Zuph, an Ephraimite.* ² *And he had two wives: the name of one was Hannah, and the name of the other Peninnah. Peninnah had children, but Hannah had no children.* ³ *This man went up from his city yearly to worship and sacrifice to the LORD of hosts in Shiloh. Also the two sons of Eli, Hophni and Phinehas, the priests of the LORD, were there.* ⁴ *And whenever the time came for Elkanah to make an offering, he would give portions to Peninnah his wife and to all her sons and daughters.* ⁵ *But to Hannah he would give a*

double portion, for he loved Hannah, although the LORD had closed her womb. *6* And her rival also provoked her severely, to make her miserable, because the LORD had closed her womb. *7* So it was, year by year, when she went up to the house of the LORD, that she provoked her; therefore she wept and did not eat. *8* Then Elkanah her husband said to her, "Hannah, why do you weep? Why do you not eat? And why is your heart grieved? Am I not better to you than ten sons?"

9 So Hannah arose after they had finished eating and drinking in Shiloh. Now Eli the priest was sitting on the seat by the doorpost of the tabernacle of the LORD. *10* And she was in bitterness of soul, and prayed to the LORD and wept in anguish. *11* Then she made a vow and said, "O LORD of hosts, if You will indeed look on the affliction of Your maidservant and remember me, and not forget Your maidservant, but will give Your maidservant a male child, then I will give him to the LORD all the days of his life, and no razor shall come upon his head."

12 And it happened, as she continued praying before the LORD, that Eli watched her mouth. *13* Now Hannah spoke in her heart; only her lips moved, but her voice was not heard. Therefore Eli thought she was drunk. *14* So Eli said to her, "How long will you be drunk? Put your wine away from you!"

15 But Hannah answered and said, "No, my lord, I am a woman of sorrowful spirit. I have drunk neither wine nor intoxicating drink, but have poured out my soul before the LORD. *16* Do not consider your maidservant a wicked woman, for out of the abundance of my complaint and grief I have spoken until now." *17* Then Eli answered and said, "Go in peace, and the God of Israel grant your *petition which you have asked of Him." *[18]* And she said, "Let your maidservant find favor in your sight." So the woman went her way and ate, and her face was no longer sad.* (NKJV)

There are three definitions of the word *"victim"* that are pertinent to our discussion regarding Hannah and the victim's veil. Those definitions are:

1. A person who suffers from a destructive or injurious action
2. A person who is deceived, mislead or falsely persuaded by his or her own emotions
3. A person mislead or falsely persuaded by someone else's dishonesty

Using the story of Hannah, found in I Samuel Chapter 1, as well as the preceding definitions, we will examine the victim's veil. Examining Hannah's story in this manner will help us realize when we are victims, and more importantly, help us move from victim to victor.

1. **Hannah suffered from a destructive or injurious action** every time Peninnah opened her mouth to taunt her about her barrenness (verses 6-7). Peninnah's incredibly insensitive jeering constantly reminded Hannah of her inability to have the one thing she desired most: a son. Peninnah's words cut at the very core of Hannah's self-esteem, as during those days, children were a measure of a woman's worth. It was bad enough that Hannah was a victim of circumstances over which she had no control. Peninnah's callousness was meant to destroy Hannah heaping insult upon injury which made her journey from victim to victor more difficult.

People dealing with the victim's veil must confront the veil of deception. This is so because victims often see themselves as having no way out or without hope of change. It is this distortion of truth the devil uses to reinforce the victim's veil. In Hannah's case, Peninnah's teasing threatened to keep Hannah in a state of inferiority and self-pity. Her tormenting, destructive and injurious words insinuated that Hannah's situation was hopeless and disgraceful. Hannah became a victim to her physical condition and she a victim to the words of her adversary: Penninah.

Like Hannah, we sometimes find ourselves at the receiving end of someone's insults, falling victim to injured or hurt feelings. How many negative things have we said or thought about ourselves simply because we took to heart someone else's derogatory opinion? How many people, male and female, have become the victims of destructive relationships, suffering silently? Hannah suffered at the hand of her adversary; however, we often suffer at the hand of those we love and who claim to love us. And like Hannah, we keep the hurt and anguish veiled (masked, disguised or hidden).

2. **Hannah was deceived or cheated by her own emotions**. Yearly as they went up to worship and sacrifice to the Lord, Peninnah provoked Hannah. At each provocation, Hannah measured herself by the words of her adversary. Hannah measured who she was based on what "others" thought she should be and who "she" thought she should be. Each provocation stirred in her feelings of inadequacy and inferiority, by which she judged herself. Thus, she became a victim, falsely persuaded by her own emotions. Hannah wore the victim's veil; a mask not directly expressing her thoughts, hiding the real nature of her sadness. In fact, her emotions blinded her to the depth of her husband's love

(verse 8). Her emotions coupled with Peninnah's disparaging words tormented her to the point that she derived no comfort from her husband's confession that he loved her more than ten sons. Through her emotions, Hannah could only see that she did not measure up to the customs of the times.

Today, if we are not careful, we too may get caught up in the expectations of our times. For example, some women feel inadequate because they do not have the job or live in the house dictated by today's social standards. However, women are not the only wearers of the victim's veil. There are men who, because of their physical appearance or other imperfection, court feelings of inadequacy, inferiority and low self-esteem. If we (male or female) allow those feelings to fester, we, like Hannah, risk becoming victimized by stereotypes and unreal expectations. Victimized by a veil of deception, something covering the truth; a person deceived, misled or falsely persuaded by our emotions.

3. **Hannah was also misled or falsely persuaded by someone else's dishonesty.** Peninnah was not being honest with Hannah every time she taunted her. True enough, Hannah was barren and considered a disgrace to her husband. However, Peninnah's action against Hannah was motivated by jealousy. She was in love with a man who loved someone else more. Peninnah veiled her jealousy with her ugly comments about Hannah's barrenness. In this way, she reinforced Hannah's victim mentality.

Dishonesty comes in many forms: from someone like Peninnah seeking company for her misery to someone using dishonesty to get what they want to someone simply operating in denial. However it comes, we risk putting on the victim's veil. For example, consider the woman (young or old) who engages in sexual activity because her partner dishonestly professes his love for her. She runs the risk of victimization on many levels. She risks being hurt when she finally learns the truth. She risks sexual addiction, which causes her to act without discretion. She even risks pregnancy, which could possibly keep her in victim mode for many years.

Dishonesty is not only a human characteristic. It is also typical of the society in which we live. The custom of our time, for instance, says that people should taste and see before they marry. This custom attempts to mislead us into believing something is wrong with "not" being sexually active before marriage. Lured by this deception, numerous men and women—even Christians—have succumbed to their flesh. In so doing, they became victims: victims of hurt and despair; victims of shattered dreams; victims of disillusion; victims in ways others cannot even imagine. Some of them have not yet recovered. Some of them may never recover.

If the truth were told, both Hannah and Peninnah were victims. Hannah was a victim of Peninnah's dishonesty, and Peninnah was a victim of her own jealous emotions. But the story does not end there. Although for years, Hannah suffered because of Peninnah's words, because of her own negative emotions, and because of her husband's failure to understand her grief, she did not give up. Though she concealed herself behind the victim's veil, she refused to be defeated. As a result, she eventually moved from victim to victor and incidentally provided a great example for us.

There were four things Hannah had and used that led her to a place of victory.

1. **Hannah had faith in God.** Jesus instructed His disciples to "Have faith in God" (Mark 11:22). Hannah always accompanied her husband to make their yearly sacrifice. Each time Hannah went to the temple to pray. She knew in whom she believed and she knew God was her source of strength and victory. She eventually became persuaded that He would grant her petition.

2. **Hannah was persistent.** Again, I Samuel 1:3 states that Elkanah and Hannah went up yearly to worship and sacrifice unto the Lord. We can also see the passage of time in the birth of Peninnah's children, for she had sons and daughters. From this we can deduce that Hannah did not just pray once. She didn't stop praying because nothing happened. And remember: nothing happened for years. Hannah persisted; she worshipped and prayed through her hurt and pain. She persisted until God answered her prayer, until she became a victor (See Luke 18:1-7).

3. **Hannah walked in forgiveness.** Although I Samuel does not say Hannah forgave, we know that she could not hold unforgiveness or bitterness in her heart towards Peninnah and effectively pray. Consider Mark 11:25-26, "when you stand praying, forgive if you have ought against any that your Father also which is in heaven may forgive you your trespasses. But if you don't forgive, neither will your Father which is in heaven forgive your trespasses." Hannah had to forgive Peninnah every time she opened her mouth. She had to forgive her husband every time he did not understand how she felt. She even had to forgive herself when she chose self-pity instead of trusting that God had a plan for her

51

deliverance. Had she not walked in forgiveness, she would not have walked into victory.

4. **Hannah chose to remove her veil and stop being a victim of circumstance**. When Eli the priest approached Hannah, supposing she was drunk, Hannah suddenly faced a moment of decision. She could remain silent, hiding behind her victim's veil, or she could remove the veil and expose the truth about her situation. She chose the truth. She told the priest the truth behind her actions, in turn exposing the truth about her suffering. It was only after she removed her veil that the priest made a declaration of faith regarding her situation: "the God of Israel grant thee thy petition that thou has asked of him" (I Samuel 1: 17).

At that point, things began to change. Hannah's face was no longer sad, and she was able to sit down and eat. I Samuel 1:19-20 states, "Elkanah knew Hannah his wife, and the Lord remembered her. So it came to pass in the process of time that Hannah conceived and bore a son, and called his name Samuel, saying Because I have asked for him from the Lord." There you have it. Hannah's faith, persistence, forgiveness and willingness to remove her victim's veil worked together to move her from a place of defeat to the place of victory. As time permits, read through I Samuel 2:1-11.

You might be curious as to why it took so long for Hannah to reach the place of victory. I don't really know, but verse 20 says, "it came to pass in the *process* of time" (emphasis added). One possibility is that it took Hannah time to get to the place of victory in each of the four areas previously discussed. Victory is not always automatic. It takes time to build faith, as faith comes by hearing (more than once), and persistence which indicates a repeated action. Also, forgiveness, which we must do, is a process that often takes time. If we were to examine ourselves honestly, we might discover areas where we are reluctant to remove our veils to expose the behind-the-scenes truth. But the day will come when God will confront us about our particular veil, we like Hannah will have to make a choice — stay in it or take it off. Victim or Victor: the choice is really up to you. Just remember: in Christ, you are never defeated, so why not begin your journey to victory today!

Worship

In Warfare

Elder Sharon R. Kornegay

It is a slap in the devil's face to worship God in the midst of warfare. Yet, we are going to do just that. He does not sit on the throne of our hearts; therefore, we refuse to allow him to get in the way of our worship to Almighty God.

I served in the United States Air Force during a military campaign. A military campaign denotes a time in which military forces are involved in conflict and combat operations with the enemy. Campaigns are formed with the purpose of achieving a desired resolution. A campaign may be comprised of a single battle or a series of battles over a specified period of time. Like military campaigns, our individual lives are often comprised of times of direct battle with the enemy.

In fact, when a person becomes a committed and mature Christian, he or she is often catapulted into the battle zone where warfare is imminent. The enemy sometimes assaults us with relentless and intense waves of disarming emotions, such as intimidation and frustration. These are what I refer to as shock and awe tactics, designed to disorganize and hinder our ability to rebound and move forward. However, God has endued us with the power of the Holy Spirit that we need during times of warfare (Acts 1:8). Still, there are times for all of us when we feel discouraged and weak and are tempted to faint or give up.

Even so, quitting is never an option for those who have determined in their minds to live for Christ. God did not create us to be weak-minded Christians. Rather, the Word of God admonishes us to be strong and courageous and to resist fear and discouragement because the Lord our God is with us wherever we go (Joshua 1:9). Even I have experienced times when I had to call on prayer warriors and others to stand with me in faith, thereby refusing to back down from the threats and attacks the enemy launched against me. As a unified force, we established a fortress that could not be shaken. Other times, I stood alone without the benefit of praying believers, totally reliant on God for a strategy of war. I learned that we must use different warfare strategies in order to positively impact the outcome of our situations.

One extremely important strategy of war is worship. In fact, I contend that worship is the one strategy that applies to every conflict. It is not an option if winning is our goal. The strategy of worship in warfare became invaluable to me when I accepted God's call to lead a worldwide prayer ministry. In that capacity, I immediately became one of the enemy's primary targets. I learned to use prayer, praise

56

and worship to thwart the enemy's plan every time. Worship became my obedient response to God's instructions. I realized that worship is much more than a slow song. Often, when I am most challenged, I find myself singing as well as speaking to God, lifting hands to Him in total adoration, completely lost in worship.

However, worshipping God is never without opposition. Because worship directly conflicts with the devil's intents and purposes, he spends an inordinate amount of time and uses various tactics to deter us. After all, he is quite desperate! The key then is obedience. We must commit to obey God, where worship is concerned, no matter how we feel. At the same time, we must never forsake church attendance, fellowship and Bible study, as these activities support and help us in our worship endeavors.

As worshippers, we can effectively stand against the devil. In order to stand, however, we must ensure that we put on our war clothes. If any part of the uniform is missing, the enemy will launch an attack in that area and will move us from our position of worship. The Bible is clear that we must be fully clothed with His armor in order to defeat the enemy. Ephesians 6:12-18 (NIV) states, "Therefore put on the full armor of God, so that when the day of evil comes, you may be able to stand your ground, and after you have done everything, to stand. Stand firm then, with the belt of truth buckled around your waist, with the breastplate of righteousness in place, and with your feet fitted with the readiness that comes from the gospel of peace. In addition to all this, take up the shield of faith, with which you can extinguish all the flaming arrows of the evil one. Take the helmet of salvation and the sword of the Spirit, which is the word of God. And pray in the Spirit on all occasions with all kinds of prayers and requests. With this in mind, be alert and always keep on praying for all the Lord's people."

Every part of the armor enables worship. Take away any part of the armor, and suddenly your ability to worship God is hindered. For example, the devil is an imitator. Everything he does is rooted in deception, and he will endeavor to deceive us where worship is concerned. Therefore, if your mind is not renewed with the Word of God—that is, if you are not wearing the helmet of salvation—you will fall prey to his deception, relax your position of worship, and lose your particular battle. There are examples for each piece of the armor regarding its relationship to worship. In other words, the armor of God is crucial to praise and worship, which is one of the greatest weapons a Christian can use to stand against the devil's wiles.

Please understand that we are to worship the Father in Spirit and in truth (see John 4:23-24). Our worship must not be misguided or erroneous in nature. Regardless of how much the enemy tries to terrorize us, we are to stand firm and refuse to worship the enemy in any aspect. One thing I like about the Bible is that it is a show-and-tell guide. It doesn't just tell us how to live, but it also shows us how to live (and incidentally how not to live as well). Along those lines, we will examine how several Biblical characters successfully responded to warfare with worship.

In II Chronicles 20, Jehoshaphat provides an excellent example of what it means to worship in warfare. Confronted with an assault from three unified armies, Jehoshaphat resolved to inquire of the Lord. However, his inquiry did not merely consist of asking; it was heavily laced with worship. Pay careful attention to his words: "O Lord, God of our fathers, are you not the God who is in heaven? You rule over all the kingdoms of the nations. Power and might are in your hand, and no one can withstand you. O our God, did you not drive out the inhabitants of this land before your people Israel and give it forever to the descendants of Abraham your friend? If calamity comes upon us, whether the sword of judgment, or plague or famine, we will stand in your presence before this temple that bears your Name and will cry out to you in our distress, and you will hear and save us" (II Chronicles 20: 6-7, 9 NIV).

In his worship, Jehoshaphat did three things that are attributes of worship and that guarantee victory in warfare. First, Jehoshaphat personalized his connection to God. He moved from seeing God as the God of his fathers (verse 6) to being his God (verse 7). This is important because it signifies relationship, and true and effective praise flows only from a personal relationship with God (the object of our worship). Second, Jehoshaphat's words of worship focused on the virtues of the Father and not the situation. In so doing, they elevated God over his problem and consequently put him in a place of victory. Finally, in verse 9, Jehoshaphat established his commitment—that of prayer during affliction—and his confident expectation—help from God in time of need. Basically, when things looked grim for Jehoshaphat so much that he did not know what to do, he bowed with his face to the ground and worshipped God. He and the people of Judah knew that the battle belonged to the Lord. Sure enough, God set ambushes against his enemies, and they were defeated!

Esther also realized that worship is a potent force, especially when employed against the enemy. She responded to warfare by calling a fast and thereby successfully stood against her adversary, Haman. In the midst of her distress, she assessed the situation and came up with a strategic plan. Thus, she did not face her enemy unprepared. I just believe that she knew deep down on the inside that the fast would move the hand of God. She had to be thoroughly convinced that He would come through, for she declared, "If I perish, I perish, but I am going to see the King" (Esther 4:16). Sure enough, God flipped the script on Haman, and Esther came out victoriously.

For another worship-in-warfare example, let's look at Shadrach, Meshach and Abednego's response to warfare. In Daniel 3, these three men refused to bow down and worship King Nebuchadnezzar's golden monument, erected to honor the king. Their response was in direct conflict with King Nebuchadnezzar's desire for them to worship his idol. They knew in whom they believed. They too responded with fasting.

Their worship response is recorded in the Daniel 3: 16-18: "O Nebuchadnezzar, we do not need to defend ourselves before you in this matter. If we are thrown into the blazing furnace, the God we serve is able to save us from it, and he will rescue us from your hand, O king. But even if he does not, we want you to know, O king, that we will not serve your gods or worship the image of gold you have set up." Their refusal to bow to Nebuchadnezzar's image was not based on God's deliverance. They refused to worship the image because they were committed to worshipping the only true God. You will also do well to remember that there is no worship without commitment.

Their worship angered Nebuchadnezzar, as worship often stirs up the enemy. Consequently, the king ordered the furnace heated seven times hotter before having the three tossed in. In fact, it was so hot that it killed the soldiers, as they threw the three into the furnace (Daniel 3:22). However, it does not matter how stirred up the enemy gets, if you stay committed to worship, you will overcome. Shortly after the young men were cast into the furnace, Nebuchadnezzar made a startling discovery: "he said to his counselors, Did not we cast three men bound into the midst of the fire? Lo, I see four men loose, walking in the midst of the fire, and they have no hurt; and the form of the fourth is like the Son of God" (Daniel 3:24-25 KJV). Nebuchadnezzar discovered what the three men already knew: that worship brings God on the scene, and He always brings deliverance with Him. In this case, Nebuchadnezzar ordered them out of the furnace, addressing them as "servants of the Most High God" (verse 26). When they came out, "the fire had not harmed their bodies, nor was a hair of their heads singed; their robes were not scorched, and there was no smell of fire on them" (verse 27). I am here to tell you that, because of worship, God came through for those young men. And He will also come through for us.

How did Jesus respond to warfare? In Matthew 4:8-9 (NIV), "the devil took him to a very high mountain and showed him all the kingdoms of the world and their splendor [and said] All this I will give you if you will bow down and worship me." Jesus responded from his position of worship: "Away from you, Satan! For it is written: Worship the Lord your God, and serve Him only." Jesus is our ultimate example. He shows us that God commands us to worship Him. In fact, the Bible says that the Father seeks those who will worship Him in Spirit and in truth. We cannot respond to His commandments in a lukewarm manner. He is our Heavenly Father and deserves so much more than that.

Again, I must emphasize that worship is more than a slow song. It begins and ends with a response from the heart. We worship the Father in Spirit and in truth by being obedient to that which He has called, anointed, appointed and purposed for us to do. We must not be intimidated or fear the enemy. Greater is He that is in us than he that is in the world. We must respond to warfare in the authority of the name of Jesus Christ. There is still power in His name. The enemy was boasting to Jesus about the things of the world. He failed to realize that Jesus already owns everything that he was trying to offer to Him, as revealed in Colossians 1: 16: " For by him all things were created: things in heaven and on earth, visible and invisible, whether thrones or powers or rulers or authorities; all things were created by Him and for Him."

In essence, the devil does not have any new tricks. We must be consistent in our worship to God. In the midst of trials and tribulations, we must remain solid in faith. The point of this chapter is to encourage you to dedicate your life to worship God in the midst of warfare. None of us are exempt from warfare, but God has given us the strategies that we need in order to be successful. We have the power to command the devil to untie our hands and unshackle our feet. Through the blood of Jesus Christ, we have victory. Sometimes we may have to cry. Nevertheless, we must determine in our hearts to stand up, dust ourselves off and begin to worship God in the midst of the warfare. Why? Because worship in warfare always ensures victory!

REMOVING *The* Veil | ABOUT THE AUTHORS

CARRADINE FRANKLIN HAWKINS KORNEGAY PINKNEY

Co-Pastor Brenda Carradine accepted Jesus Christ as Lord and Savior on 9 Aug 1980. She was called to ministry in 1993; ordained as an Elder with CHSC, Inc. and set in the office as Co-pastor, assisting her husband in their first pastor-ship in Tokyo, Japan in 1998. As a gifted orator and woman of God, she has travelled ministering in women conferences throughout the world. She is the founder of the Palm of Deborah women's ministry, and is a published author. *Lady Preacher* is her first published work, and she is currently working on her second book entitled *Silly Women*. Brenda holds a Bachelors of Science degree in Nursing from Texas Christian University and a Masters degree in Public Administration from Troy State University.

She is married to Bishop Ernest E. Carradine, Sr. and has been blessed with twenty-four years of marriage and five children: Jonathan (22), Megan (20), Keisha (20), and the twins Ernest Jr. and Whitney (13). Together Bishop and 1st Lady Carradine have carried the Gospel of Jesus Christ to locations such as Japan, United Kingdom, Germany, Italy, Bulgaria, Guam, Netherlands, Iceland, Austria and various places across the United States. Their heart's desire is to see the Body of Christ walk in Godly maturity in word and deed, according to Ephesians 4:12-13, pushing Kingdom agenda throughout the world. It is for this reason they are called.

Evangelist Yolanda Franklin serves as Secretary for World Intercessory Network and is currently employed by the SAIC where she is a Project Accounting/Control Manager. She is also an entrepreneur, managing several businesses such as Daycare, Rental Property, Destiny Graphics and Franklin Financial. She graduated with honors from Middle Georgia Technical College with a Certificate of Business Administration. Yolanda also received an Associates of Business Administration from both Middle Georgia College and Macon State College and received her Bachelor's Degree in Accounting at Macon State College. Yolanda was recognized in Who's Who Among Black Business Women, and she is a member of several Accounting Associations.

Yolanda married Pastor Larry Franklin Jr. They are blessed with four daughters: Brittany, Le'Shaunda, Eboni, and Diamond. She is a faithful member of Nazarene Church of God in Christ. She is a licensed Missionary, Sunday School Teacher, and President of the Women's Department, Board of Trustees, and Secretary. She is active at her church organization's district level as well. She serves as the District Finance Chairperson and Chairlady to the District Missionary. She loves teaching and doing evangelistic work for the Lord.

Elder Karen Hawkins is the founder and president of Vessels Unto Honor, Inc. She also serves as Vice President/Treasurer of the World Intercessory Network, Inc. Her goal is to see women, across the Body of Christ, stand virtuous, lovely and precious in the sight of God. With a desire to see others come to know the Lord Jesus Christ, the Lord has anointed her to teach the Word of God with love and demonstration of His power.

Karen is a native New Yorker. She has one daughter, Theresa, who lives in Montgomery, AL. Karen retired after 32 years of federal civil service while living in Eastpointe, Michigan where she was a member of Family Victory Fellowship Church. She is a graduate and instructor in the Ambassador Bible Training School, Southfield, Michigan. Karen was first ordained an Elder in the African Methodist Episcopal Zion Church after finishing four years of liturgical studies. She is currently ordained under Compassionate Christian Center Church, Santa Maria, California serving under Pastors Elvie and Jackie Jackson. She has a Bachelor's Degree in Business Administration from Northwood University. Karen served on the ministerial staff at Mt. Zion AME Zion Church, Montgomery, AL, Lompoc Church, Lompoc, CA, and served as Pastor at Matthews Chapel AME Zion Church in Cecil, AL. Karen has relocated back to Montgomery, Alabama and is now a member of Better Covenant Ministries under Pastors Andre and Valerie Prude.

Elder Sharon Kornegay is President and Founder of World Intercessory Network Inc (W.I.N.) and Ladies Intercessory Praise Sessions (L.I.P.S). She accepted Jesus Christ as Lord and Savior at a young age and re-dedicated her life to Christ in October 1986

She totally yielded to the call of God on January 25, 1998, in Lompoc, CA, under the leadership of Pastor Elvie Jackson. Upon relocating to Warner Robins, GA, she served as a music minister, youth minister, youth choir leader, volunteered in the prison and nursing home ministries, and at a local soup kitchen. Her passion is to reach broken and hurting women. She firmly stands on Luke 4:18, "Jesus came to heal the broken-hearted." She is employed with the federal government. She has traveled both nationally and internationally, spreading the Gospel of Jesus Christ. She is committed to the call to pray and to serve as a bridge to unite brothers and sisters together as one body of believers

World Intercessory Network was birthed when she and one of her Christian sisters began using the Internet to pray for each other. She holds a degree in General Studies from Georgia Military College, a Paralegal Fundamentals Certificate from Middle Georgia Technical College and is completing a degree in Criminal Justice and Public Service at Macon State College. Born and raised in Bessemer, AL, she and her husband Joey now reside in Warner Robins, Georgia with their three children.

Co-Pastor Kimberly Pinkney serves on the Board of Directors for the World Intercessory Network and as President of the Ladies Intercessory Praise Sessions-Warner Robins, GA. She accepted Jesus Christ as her personal Savior at the age of 8. She also experienced the healing power of God in her body after being delivered and healed from epilepsy, juvenile arthritis, hypoglycemia and ulcers. Kimberly has been walking in that freedom for over 22 years. Therefore, she has developed a passion for people being set free from any bondage

Kimberly is co-founder of Spirit of Victory Church (SOVC) serving with her husband, Pastor Robert Pinkney. Kimberly co-authored the book, *Out of the Closet and Into God's Love*, which is a testimonial that chronicles the Pinkneys' personal and life-changing encounter with the delivering power of God. Kimberly and her husband publish an e-newsletter, *Victory Truths*, providing readers with world-overcoming truths. They also founded Victorious Living Ministries, with the goal of bringing Biblical teaching, tools and the deliverance to anyone struggling with homosexuality. The Pinkneys are also involved in marriage ministry aimed at teaching husbands and wives how to walk out the God-kind of marriage. The Pinkneys have been married for 20 years and reside in Bonaire, Georgia, and have four children.

Kimberly holds an Associate of Science in Business Administration from Georgia Military College and a certificate from the International Training in Communication in public speaking and currently works for the Houston County School Board as a substitute teacher.

The authors of this book would like to thank you for your interest and support. They invite you to visit them online for updates on more extraordinary works to come.

WWW.TAKINGOFFTHEMASK.COM

The publisher of this book would like to thank you for your support. You are invited to visit the link below, should you desire information regarding publishing services.

WWW.HARRISPUBCO.COM

Notes

Notes